Project

Bugs

THE PROJECT MAKERS

Camilla de la Bédoyère

WINDMILL BOOKS

D0845679

Published in 2020 by Windmill Books, an imprint of Rosen Publishing 29 East 21ˢᵗ Street, New York, NY 10010

Copyright © 2020 Miles Kelly Publishing

All rights reserved. No part of this book may be reproduced in any form without permission in writing from the publisher, except by a reviewer.

Publishing Director: Belinda Gallagher
Creative Director: Jo Cowan
Senior Editor: Fran Bromage
Designers: Joe Jones, Andrea Slane
Cover Design: Simon Lee
Consultant: Steve Parker
Indexer: Marie Lorimer
Image Manager: Liberty Newton
Production: Elizabeth Collins, Caroline Kelly
Reprographics: Stephan Davis, Jennifer Cozens
Assets: Lorraine King

Cataloging-in-Publication Data

Names: de la Bédoyère, Camilla.
Title: Project bugs / Camilla de la Bédoyère.
Description: New York : Windmill Books, 2020. | Series: The project makers | Includes index.
Identifiers: ISBN 9781538392263 (pbk.) | ISBN 9781725393035 (library bound) | ISBN 9781538392270 (6 pack)
Subjects: LCSH: Insects--Juvenile literature. | Handicraft--Juvenile literature.
Classification: LCC QL467.2 D445 2019 | DDC 595.7--dc23

Manufactured in the United States of America

CPSIA Compliance Information: Batch #BW20WM:
For Further Information contact Rosen Publishing,
New York, New York at 1-800-237-9932

How to use the projects

This book is packed full of awesome facts about bugs. There are also 11 cool projects, designed to make the subject come alive.

Before you start a project:

• Always ask an adult to help you.

• Read the instructions carefully.

• Gather all the supplies you need.

• Clear a surface to work on and cover it with newspaper.

• Wear an apron or old T-shirt to protect your clothing.

Notes for helpers:

• Children will need supervision for the projects, usually because they require the use of scissors, or preparation beforehand.

• Read the instructions together before starting and help to gather the equipment.

IMPORTANT NOTICE
The publisher and author cannot be held responsible for any injuries, damage, or loss resulting from the use or misuse of any of the information in this book.

SAFETY FIRST!
Be careful when using glue or anything sharp, such as scissors. Always wash your hands after handling bugs and remember that some bugs may bite or sting.

How to use:
If your project doesn't work the first time, try again – just have fun!

Butterfly prints

Supplies:
The equipment should be easy to find, around the house or from a craft store. Always ask before using materials from home.

Numbered stages:
Each stage of the project is numbered. Follow the stages in the order shown to complete the project. If glue or paint is used, make sure it is dry before moving on to the next stage.

Create your own perfect print of a butterfly. Butterflies are symmetrical. This means that if you look at a butterfly from above you will see that the two halves of its body look exactly the same.

SUPPLIES
three different colors of paint • thin paintbrushes • paper

HOW TO MAKE
1. Fold the paper in half and open it out again.

2. On one side, use your first color to paint the basic shape of the butterfly.

3. Quickly fold the paper in half again and press it down so the paint makes a print on the second side.

4. Open the paper and let your print dry.

5. Now paint with your second color and repeat the pressing and printing.

6. After it's dried, use your third color.

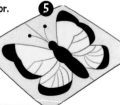

Most other bugs are symmetrical, too. Can you make prints of some other bugs you like from this book?

CONTENTS

Join the Bug Club

Step outside and take a walk on the wild side, where amazing mini monsters hunt and creepy-crawlies roam. This is the land of bugs and there are plenty of exciting discoveries to be made. Are you ready to become a sharp-eyed, curious, and brilliant bug detective?

WHAT IS A BUG?

Most people use the word bug to refer to insects and creepy-crawlies, but scientists use bug to describe a group of insects with special sucking mouthparts.

BONELESS WONDERS

Bugs are invertebrates, which means they belong to a huge group of animals that don't have bones. Types of invertebrate you might find on a nature trek include: insects, spiders, worms, crustaceans (such as crabs and woodlice), and mollusks (such as slugs and snails).

Bugs are all shapes and colors. A Colorado beetle's stripes warn birds that it tastes bad.

This red wood ant is actually between .2 and .4 inch (5 and 9 mm) in length.

FINDING BUGS

The best place to look for bugs is outdoors, but some of them like living in buildings. Most bugs are small, and most of them live in soil, wood, ponds, under stones, and around plants, so these are the best places to start looking.

A mini home made from bamboo can be hung from trees to help bees nest and stay snug in winter.

Remember that some bugs bite or sting, so always take care. Do not annoy bees and wasps and never try to touch them.

What does that mean?

Here are some useful words.

Exoskeleton
A tough outer skin

Habitat
The place where an animal or plant lives

Metamorphosis
A big change in body shape

Nectar
A sugary liquid in flowers

Nymph
A young insect that looks like the adult

Predator
An animal that hunts other animals to eat

Prey
An animal hunted by other animals

Proboscis
A long mouthpart used to suck up liquids

Pupa
A hard-cased stage in insect metamorphosis

Start investigating bugs!

Bug collectors need a pooter. It's a simple piece of equipment that's easy to make.

SUPPLIES

see-through jars or plastic pots • bendy straws • sticky tack or plasticine • old tights or muslin • small rubber band • scissors or a nail

HOW TO MAKE

1. Ask an adult to help you make two holes in the lid with scissors or a nail. Push a straw through each hole.

2. Use sticky tack to secure the straws and fill any spaces around the holes.

3. Tie a tiny piece of the tights to the bottom end of one straw and secure it with the rubber band. This is important because it will prevent you from sucking a bug into your mouth!

HOW TO USE

Find a bug, then place the end of straw A right next to it. Suck into straw B and the bug will be pulled up, through straw A, into the pooter, where you can examine it. When you have finished examining your bug, release it outside and remember to wash your hands.

Straw B   Straw A

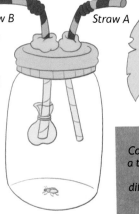

Collect one bug at a time, or separate the bugs into different pots once you've caught them.

See page 14 for Body Basics.

5

Creepy-crawlies

Bugs are famous for creeping and crawling, but they have plenty of other ways to get around. They can run, walk, climb, fly, swim, scamper, float, squirm, wriggle, slither, and scurry! Like other animals, they move to get food, to escape from danger, and to find a mate.

LOVELY LEGS

Bugs have lots of uses for their many legs. Grasshoppers' legs are perfect for leaping away from danger. Spiders use their legs to spin webs. A dung beetle's legs are great for rolling lumps of dung!

Dragonflies can hover above water and use their long legs to pluck out prey.

SPEEDY SKATERS

Pond skaters scoot across the surface of a pond. They use their middle legs to row forward, their hind legs to steer, and the front pair of legs to grab their food.

Sensitive hairs on a pond skater's legs help it to detect vibrations on the water's surface created by other bugs.

Walking on water

Discover how some bugs can walk on water.

SUPPLIES

bowl of water • paper clips • paper towel

WHAT TO DO

1. Put the paper clip in the bowl and watch it sink.

2. Carefully place a piece of paper towel on the surface of the water.

3. Gently put a paper clip on the paper towel.

4. Slowly push the paper towel to the bottom of the bowl, without disturbing the paper clip. Now the paper clip will stay on the surface of the water.

1

The paper clip sinks because, like a bug, it's heavier than water.

2

The paper floats because it's lighter than the water it's resting on.

3

The paper clip floats because the paper supports it.

4

Now the paper clip will stay on the surface of the water.

What, how, why?

Water is made up of tiny units called molecules that pull or attract each other, especially at the surface of a liquid. This stickiness is called surface tension. The paper clip isn't floating, it's being held up by the surface tension of the water molecules. They hold on to each other to create an invisible "sheet".

Dishwashing liquid reduces surface tension. How can you prove this?

SUPER SLIME

Snails and slugs use sticky slime to slither along the undersides of leaves, where birds can't see them. Some burrowing invertebrates, including worms, cover their bodies with slime to slip through soil.

HIGH FLIERS

A flying bug has one or two pairs of wings. The wings move up and down and to and fro, lifting it up and moving it forward. The fastest and most skillful flyers of the insect world are dragonflies. They move each wing independently, so they can also hover.

How high can a flea jump?

A cat flea can jump 12 inches (30 cm) — more than 150 times its own length.

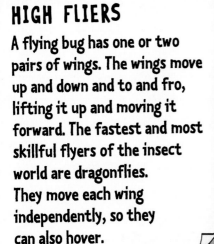

It owes its super-springiness to its legs, which work like catapults to fling it in the air.

Fleas need to jump to get from one host (an animal that they live on) to another. Once there, they can suck its blood and lay eggs.

Water world

A pond, lake, or river is a perfect place to watch bugs. Some insects, such as dragonflies, spend much of their lives as larvae under the water. Others buzz, hover, and swoop above the water, or lay their eggs on plants around the edge.

DEEP BREATHING

Diving beetles come to the surface to breathe but they also swim with bubbles of air under their wing cases. Mosquito larvae hang upside down from the surface, with two tubes poking into the air.

Mosquito larvae

BACKSWIMMERS

Water boatmen are also known as backswimmers because of their unique swimming style. They can swim upside down, paddling with their oar-shaped, hairy hind legs, and carry bubbles of air under their wings.

Giant diving beetle

Water boatmen

Caddis fly larvae

What is wrapped up in this case of grit and wood?

Pond-dipping

The best way to watch water bugs is to temporarily take them out of a pond and put them somewhere safe, away from the water's edge.

SUPPLIES

net • bucket or tray of water • notepad • magnifying lens • small ruler • pencils

WHAT TO DO

1. Stand or kneel in a safe place at a pond's edge, holding the net. Look for bugs in the water before you begin.

2. Gently sweep the net across the surface of the water, making a figure eight, to scoop up any bugs.

3. Carefully empty the net into the bucket and move it away from the pond so you can safely look at what you've caught.

4. Use your other equipment to investigate the bugs. Note their size, color, and shape, and make drawings.

5. Return the bugs gently to their pond home.

6. Back home, you can use books or the Internet to identify your bugs and find out more about them.

Always remember to wash your hands after pond-dipping.

Dragonfly nymphs can spend up to five years in a pond, but adult dragonflies will live just a few weeks.

① A female dragonfly lays its eggs on pond plants, or in water.

② When the eggs hatch, tiny wriggling larvae emerge.

③ The larvae grow and molt to become hungry underwater nymphs.

A giant water bug jabs its dagger-like mouthparts into a frog.

FEARSOME BUGS

At 4 inches (10 cm) long, giant water bugs are big enough to catch frogs and fish. They inject toxic spit into their prey, dissolving the flesh so it can be sucked up like soup!

All change

Bugs are incredible creatures because they go through an amazing change to become adults. It's called metamorphosis, a Greek word that means to change shape. Insects are the ultimate transformers of the animal kingdom — changing not just their appearance, but their lifestyles, and even habitats.

Complete metamorphosis

After complete metamorphosis, the adult looks different than the young insect and will often eat different food.

1. An egg hatches into a larva

2. A larva grows and turns into a pupa

3. A pupa turns into an adult

Simple metamorphosis

The adult looks similar to the young insect, and often lives in the same habitat.

1. An egg hatches into a nymph

2. A nymph eats, grows, and molts several times

3. After a final molt, the nymph is an adult

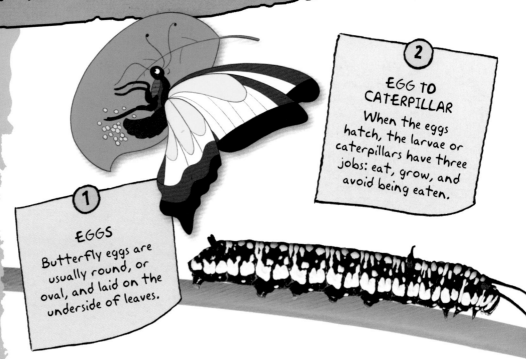

2

EGG TO CATERPILLAR
When the eggs hatch, the larvae or caterpillars have three jobs: eat, grow, and avoid being eaten.

1

EGGS
Butterfly eggs are usually round, or oval, and laid on the underside of leaves.

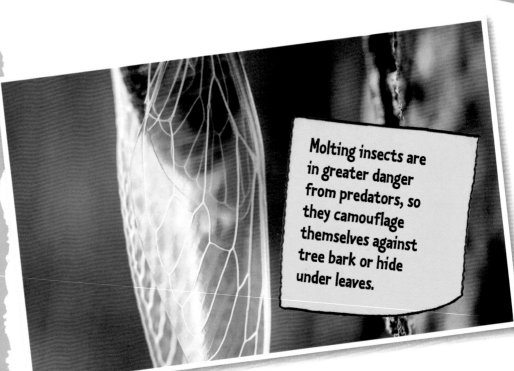

Molting insects are in greater danger from predators, so they camouflage themselves against tree bark or hide under leaves.

3 CATERPILLAR TO PUPA

As a caterpillar grows, it spins a silken case around itself (a pupa) or grows a harder skin, called a chrysalis.

4 PUPA TO BUTTERFLY

Inside the pupa or chrysalis, the caterpillar is dissolved and reforms as a butterfly.

Butterflies, like this common tiger butterfly, go through complete metamorphosis.

5 EMERGING BUTTERFLY

It takes between 30 minutes and 2 hours before the butterfly's wings are dry and it's ready to fly.

Butterfly prints

Create your own perfect print of a butterfly. Butterflies are symmetrical. This means that if you look at a butterfly from above you will see that the two halves of its body look exactly the same.

SUPPLIES
three different colors of paint
• thin paintbrushes • paper

HOW TO MAKE

1. Fold the paper in half and open it out again.

2. On one side, use your first color to paint the basic shape of the butterfly.

3. Quickly fold the paper in half again and press it down so the paint makes a print on the second side.

4. Open the paper and let your print dry.

5. Now paint with your second color and repeat the pressing and printing.

6. After it's dried, use your third color.

Most other bugs are symmetrical, too. Can you make prints of some other bugs you like from this book?

Beastly bugs

Forget lions, wolves, and sharks — the micro world of bugs is just as ferocious and deadly. Bugs need to eat, and while many of them munch plants, others have lethal weapons to trap, catch, and kill.

WASP ATTACK

A female ichneumon wasp injects her egg into the body of a beetle larva, where it hatches. The grub then eats the larva from the inside out! These wasps can help control pests, including the beetles that kill trees and crops.

PRAYING ON PREY

A praying mantis hides on a plant and waits motionless until an unsuspecting victim walks by. It uses its folded front legs to thrust forward and grab its prey, crushing it and pulling it into its mouth. The whole attack lasts less than 0.01 second!

A mantis has superb eyesight and can judge distances well, so its aim is perfect as it launches an attack.

ASSASSIN BUGS

These bugs grab onto prey with sticky pads on their legs. They use piercing mouthparts to inject venom, which turns the victim's insides to liquid.

Disappearing aphids

Ladybugs are mini predators that live in most gardens. Discover what happens when a ladybug encounters aphids!

SUPPLIES

see-through jar • old tights or muslin • rubber band • ladybug, aphids, and leaves

HOW to make the aphids disappear

1. Pinch off part of a plant that is covered with aphids.

2. Put it into the jar, along with a ladybug. Count the aphids.

3. Cover the jar top with the old tights or muslin, and secure the cloth with the rubber band.

4. After two hours, count the aphids again.

5. Count the aphids again four hours later, and one day later. Release the ladybug outside.

What, how, why?

Did all of the aphids disappear? What happened to them? Why do gardeners like ladybugs?

Ant attack

FIRE ANTS
Working as a team of up to 250,000 ants, these insects eat anything they find.

TRAPJAW ANTS
These fast ants are record breakers. Their jaws can close around a victim 2,000 times faster than a blink of an eye!

BULLET ANTS
One brave scientist got lots of ants, bees, and wasps to sting him to see which hurt most! He decided that bullet ants had the worst stings.

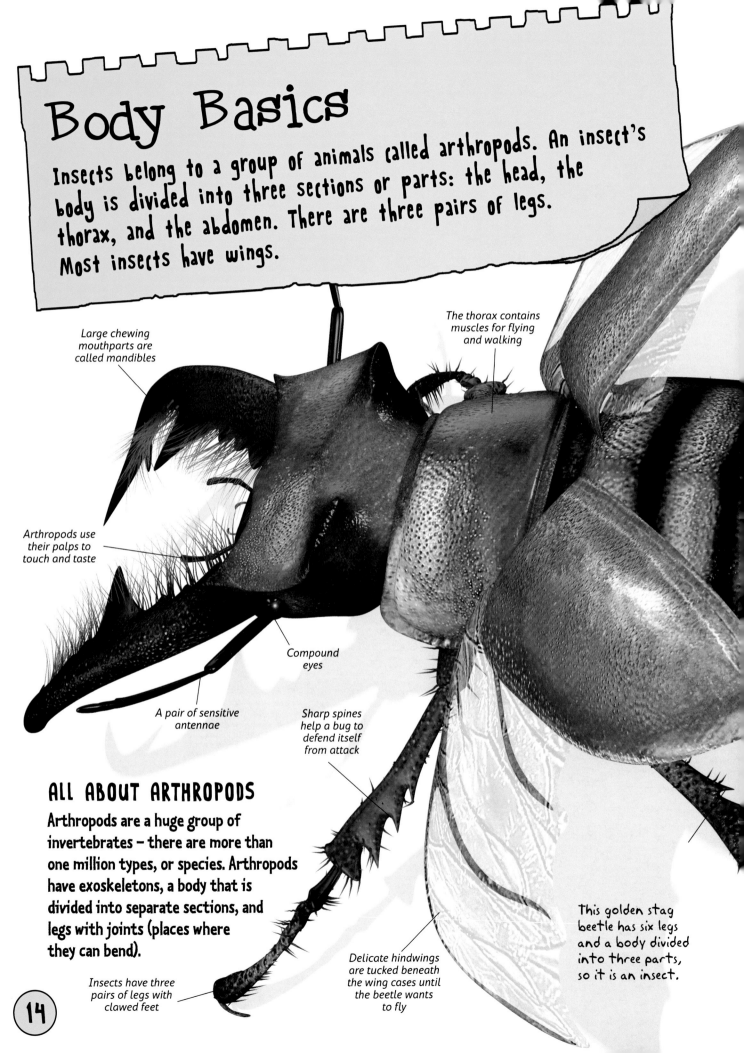

Body Basics

Insects belong to a group of animals called arthropods. An insect's body is divided into three sections or parts: the head, the thorax, and the abdomen. There are three pairs of legs. Most insects have wings.

Large chewing mouthparts are called mandibles

The thorax contains muscles for flying and walking

Arthropods use their palps to touch and taste

Compound eyes

A pair of sensitive antennae

Sharp spines help a bug to defend itself from attack

ALL ABOUT ARTHROPODS

Arthropods are a huge group of invertebrates – there are more than one million types, or species. Arthropods have exoskeletons, a body that is divided into separate sections, and legs with joints (places where they can bend).

Insects have three pairs of legs with clawed feet

Delicate hindwings are tucked beneath the wing cases until the beetle wants to fly

This golden stag beetle has six legs and a body divided into three parts, so it is an insect.

14

A KEY TO LIFE

Animal experts use keys, like this one below, to work out what type of animal they are looking at. Use a magnifying glass to closely examine your bugs, and follow the key to identify them.

Use the Internet and books to find out more about the bugs you are interested in.

A beetle's forewings are hardened. They create a protective wing case.

Little hairs on the surface of a bug help it to sense touch and movement. These hairs are called setae.

The last section, behind the thorax, is called an abdomen

The strong outer skin, or exoskeleton, protects the bug's body and all the soft parts inside

Does the invertebrate have...

Six legs (Insects)

Eight or more legs

Eight legs

Spiders Mites Scorpions Ticks

Wings

No wings

More than eight legs

Two legs on each body segment

One pair

Two pairs

Fleas Lice Bristletails Springtails Silverfish

Four legs on each body segment

Flies (such as houseflies, mosquitoes, gnats)

Millipedes

Woodlice Centipedes

Forewings are hard or leathery

Sucking mouthparts

True bugs

All wings are soft

Chewing mouthparts

Hard forewings

Wings are transparent

Earwigs Beetles

Wings covered in scales or hairs

Mayflies Stoneflies Dragonflies Scorpionflies Lacewings Bees Wasps Ants Cicadas Hoppers Aphids Termites

Leathery forewings

Scales

Hairs

Caddisflies

Cockroaches Crickets Grasshoppers Mantids Stick insects

Butterflies and moths

Record breakers!

Bugs come in all shapes and sizes. Explore some extreme and extraordinary bugs, from the world's biggest creepy-crawlies to the breathtaking beauty of giant butterflies.

Giant millipedes can grow longer than your arm!

BIGGEST FLY

The giant mydas fly lives in South America and females are larger than males. The largest specimen found had a wingspan of 4.6 inches (11.7 cm) and a body length of 2.3 inches (5.8 cm).

Adult female giant mydas flies never eat, while males suck nectar.

ACTUAL SIZE

LARGEST MILLIPEDE

This giant black millipede can grow longer than 15 inches (38 cm), but it doesn't have the most legs. An American millipede holds that record, with 750 legs!

LARGEST BUTTERFLY

The Queen Alexandra birdwing butterfly has a record-breaking wingspan of 10.6 inches (27 cm). It also has one of the world's heaviest caterpillars, which is poisonous and grows to more than 4 inches (10 cm) long.

A male Queen Alexandra birdwing butterfly. Females are not so colorful.

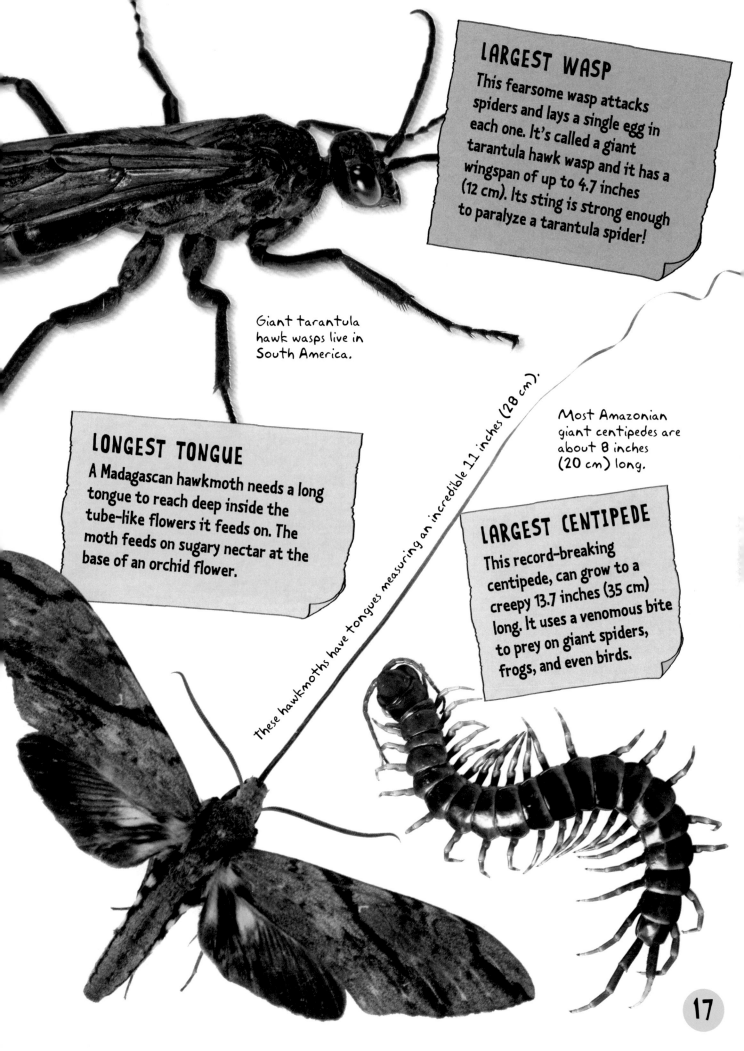

LARGEST WASP

This fearsome wasp attacks spiders and lays a single egg in each one. It's called a giant tarantula hawk wasp and it has a wingspan of up to 4.7 inches (12 cm). Its sting is strong enough to paralyze a tarantula spider!

Giant tarantula hawk wasps live in South America.

LONGEST TONGUE

A Madagascan hawkmoth needs a long tongue to reach deep inside the tube-like flowers it feeds on. The moth feeds on sugary nectar at the base of an orchid flower.

These hawkmoths have tongues measuring an incredible 11 inches (28 cm).

Most Amazonian giant centipedes are about 8 inches (20 cm) long.

LARGEST CENTIPEDE

This record-breaking centipede, can grow to a creepy 13.7 inches (35 cm) long. It uses a venomous bite to prey on giant spiders, frogs, and even birds.

BIGGEST BEETLE

Measuring up to 6.6 inches (17 cm) long, Hercules beetles are the world's longest horned beetles. These beetles also have massive maggots!

Males use their long horns to battle each other at mating time.

Giant water bugs can reach nearly 7 inches (18 cm) in length.

HEAVIEST BUG

Most water bugs are big and beefy, but the giant water bug is a real heavyweight at .88 ounce (25 g). It is a fearless predator of tadpoles and fish, and a record-breaking true bug. True bugs are insects with piercing and sucking mouthparts.

These cockroaches dig in sandy soil.

HEAVIEST COCKROACH

Weighing up to 1.2 ounces (33 g), the rhinoceros cockroach is 300 times heavier than a domestic pest cockroach. This species lives in burrows.

A record-breaking queen termite can grow to 4.7 inches (12 cm) long.

ACTUAL SIZE

Other record breakers

The largest moth is the white witch moth with a wingspan of 12 inches (30.5 cm).

The fastest insect on land is the Australian tiger beetle. It speeds along at 8.2 feet (2.5 m) a second.

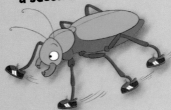

The fastest-flying fly is the deer botfly at 2.4 miles (39 km) per hour.

The longest stick insect is Chan's megastick. It measures 14 inches (35.7 cm).

BIGGEST TERMITE

This may look like a giant maggot, but it's a queen war-like termite. Her job is to lay all the eggs for her colony. She will lay millions of eggs in her lifetime.

DEADLIEST FLEA

The Oriental rat flea helps to spread deadly plagues, causing many millions of human deaths. It transmits plague when it bites its victims.

Oriental rat fleas feed on the blood of rats and humans.

LARGEST CADDISFLIES

Giant case-making caddisflies can have wingspans of 2.4 inches (6 cm). Their larvae live in water and disguise themselves with cases made of bits of plant material.

Disguising yourself, like a caddisfly larva does, is called camouflage.

Butterflies migrate to avoid cold winters.

MOST NATURALLY WIDESPREAD INSECT

The painted lady butterfly is a powerful flyer, and can cross continents and oceans. It has not yet conquered Australia, New Zealand, or Antarctica, though.

19

Defend or die

Bugs use some extremely clever tricks to avoid being eaten — from stink bombs to cunning disguises. These survival strategies can save a bug's life, so it doesn't become a juicy snack for predators, such as other invertebrates, birds, reptiles, and amphibians.

The bombardier beetle's puff of burning gas is fired out of a hole in its rear end.

KEY

1 Toxin-producing gland
2 One of two storage reservoirs
3 Enzyme-producing gland
4 Explosive chamber

BOTTOM BLAST!
Although it is often less than .4 inch (1 cm) long, the bombardier beetle wins the award for being the world's most explosive insect. When threatened, it relies on chemical warfare to provide time to escape.

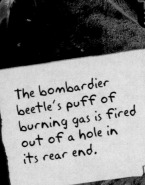

Survival tactics

FALSE COLORS
Harmless hoverflies look like wasps to fool predators into thinking they will sting.

Foul taste
Some bugs store the poison from the plants they eat, so they taste disgusting to predators, like rodents.

What a stink!
Fat and juicy stinkbugs are an easy target for birds, but they release a stinky liquid when attacked.

BLOODY-NOSED BEETLE

One of the most bizarre tricks is performed by a bloody-nosed beetle as it tries to avoid attack. It releases drops of bright red liquid from its jaws. Birds are confused by this strange event, and steer clear.

The "blood" looks scary, and it tastes bad.

Leaf insects are masters of disguise.

MIMICRY AND CAMOUFLAGE

Some bugs pretend to be something else to avoid being eaten. Stick insects mimic sticks, leaf insects pretend to be leaves, and dung crab spiders look like bird poop! The patterns and colors of a bug can help it to hide. This is called camouflage. Sometimes bugs can be brightly colored to scare off predators, too.

Create a caterpillar

Make a bright, colorful, wriggly caterpillar – and no predator will want to come close!

SUPPLIES

large egg carton • scissors • string • paints • pens • pipe cleaners

HOW TO MAKE

1. Cut the egg carton so you have lots of egg "cups" and make holes in each cup. Use string to connect them into a caterpillar body.

2. Decide how you would like your caterpillar's colors and patterns to look, and start decorating!

3. Draw on big eyes and use pipe cleaners to make bendy antennae.

21

Sensational bugs

Our senses connect us to the world, telling us what's going on and where everything is. Bugs have senses, too. Unlike humans, they have feelers on their heads, and many insects are far more sensitive to sights and smells than we are.

SUPER SCENTS

Insects communicate using chemicals called pheromones. These super scents give other bugs information, such as a warning of danger or a change in behavior.

A moth's antennae work like a nose to sense smells.

Feathery antennae

Did you know?

Dragonflies have the largest eyes of any insect.

Butterflies taste with their feet.

Cicadas have ears on their stomachs.

Bees can sense the Earth's magnetic field and use it to find their way.

Crickets have ears on their legs.

Bloodsucking bugs can detect the heat given off by other animals.

Some insects that live in dark caves are blind.

FEELING GOOD

Insects have one pair of antennae, or feelers. They detect heat, touch, sound, and taste, and are extremely sensitive. Male moths have huge feathery antennae. The male emperor moth can smell a female 6.8 miles (11 km) away!

The huge, round shape of its eyes helps an insect to see in almost all directions.

Compound eye

Making pictures

Many insects have compound eyes made up of hundreds of hexagonal-shaped lenses. This type of eye is fantastic at seeing movement. Each lens helps create a single picture. All the images are then sent to the insect's brain to be turned into one big picture.

Insects look at the world differently than we do. This is how we see a flower, but how does an insect see it?

Test your senses

We rely on our sense of sight to help us understand the world. How will you and your friends cope when you can't see what you're touching?

You will need
blindfold • bowl • lots of small household objects

HOW TO PLAY
Each person collects small objects in a bowl, without showing them to anyone else. Each person in turn is blindfolded, given the bowl, and challenged to identify each object, using just their sense of touch.

Here are some suggestions for objects:

crumpled ball of foil

dry pasta/rice

small toys

bar of soap

paper clip

elastic band

key

nail file

dry teabag

leaf

pencil

Family and friends

Bugs may be small, but some types work together to rival the power and intelligence of larger animals. They are called social insects. Termites, bees, ants, and wasps can build incredible homes and organize themselves into groups with different jobs to do.

COLONIES

A colony is a group of animals that live and work together. They are often divided into groups, called castes, to perform different jobs. The colony queen lays all the eggs and is looked after by workers. Males have only one job: to mate with the queen, whose job is to lay all the eggs. Workers are often females that protect the nest and eggs.

FAMILY LIFE

Honeybees live in colonies called hives. Worker bees visit flowers to collect pollen and nectar, and make wax to build the hexagonal-shaped cells where the queen lays her eggs. Male honeybees are called drones.

Other cells are used to store honey and pollen.

Terrific termites

Termite grubs live in the center of the mound, in a maze of galleries.

Termites can create massive mounds of mud and spit — up to 30 feet (9 m) tall and 82 feet (25 m) around the base.

There are tunnels around the center, where termites grow their food — fungus that lives on rotting plants.

HONEYPOT ANTS

Worker honeypot ants feed nectar to their nestmates, called repletes. Repletes hang from the nest roof and their abdomens swell up with nectar. This becomes a food source for the colony.

Repletes swell to hundreds of times the size of their nestmates.

Termite mounds can be huge and hundreds of years old.

Hive hexagons

Discover why bees like hexagons so much.

SUPPLIES

ruler • scissors • glue or tape • lots of cardboard tubes (toilet rolls are best)

HOW TO MAKE

1. Gather some tubes together and look at the gaps they create when they are taped together.

2. Collect a few more tubes and cut across each one so it makes three equal smaller cylinders. You might need to ask a grown-up to help you measure.

3. Flatten and fold each cylinder into a Z shape to create two folds.

4. Open up the tube and reshape it at the folds to form a hexagon with six sides.

5. Repeat until you have lots of the hexagonal tubes. These are the bee cells.

6. Tape the bee cells together and see how tightly they fit together.

Look carefully. Did you notice that the hexagons fit together without any gaps, but the cylinders had big, wasted spaces between them?

Swarm!

Some bugs spend all their lives in one small habitat, while others are global explorers. There's safety in numbers, so bugs will embark on these incredible journeys in huge groups called swarms. These journeys are called migrations.

EPIC MIGRATION

A swarm of 100 million locusts can munch its way through every bit of vegetation it passes. A swarm like this can devour enough food in one day to feed 800 people for a year. A locust swarm can fly 125 miles (200 km) a day in search of plants to eat.

SUDDEN SWARMS

The nymphs of big bugs called periodical cicadas live underground for up to 17 years. At mating time, they all emerge as adults at once. The male cicadas make a deafening sound as they climb trees to call to the females.

Adult cicadas only live for a few weeks. Many of them get plucked off trees by hungry birds.

Make a solar compass

If you had to migrate north, could you find your way? Learn this simple trick and you will be able to navigate using the sun.

SUPPLIES

a sunny day • 2 straight sticks • 2 stones

HOW TO MAKE

1. Push a stick into the ground so it is upright.

2. Use a stone to mark where the tip of the stick's shadow falls on the ground.

3. Wait for about 15 minutes and you will see the stick's shadow has moved.

4. Put the second stone where the tip of the stick's shadow now falls.

5. Place the second stick along the line created by the two stones.

6. This stick marks the West-to-East line. (Your first stone is at the West end, your second stone is at the East end.)

7. Then use the compass on this page to work out where your North and South points are.

You've made your own compass!

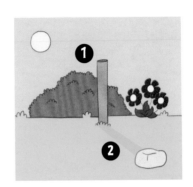

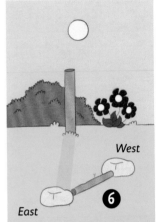

Farmers in Madagascar use nets and sheets to catch the locusts to eat.

CANADA

USA

MEXICO

Butterflies flutter by

Every year, 300 million monarch butterflies take to the skies for their annual migration.

A monarch butterfly has a frail body and flimsy wings, but it flies about 28 miles (45 km) a day during migration.

It can take several generations to make the spring migration, as they mate and lay eggs along the way.

Some butterflies fly the whole distance back again. One monarch is known to have flown 2,880 miles (4,635 km)!

Mini monsters

There are more than one million types of bugs in the world — and trillions and trillions of little critters share our planet. It's no wonder that some of them are deadly and disgusting. Meet some of the bugs that can make our lives, and those of other animals, miserable.

BLOODSUCKERS

Bloodsucking bugs include ticks, lice, mosquitoes, bed bugs, fleas, and flies. Blood makes a perfect snack for bugs that are able to pierce an animal's skin and suck it out. Some female bugs even need to feed on blood before they can lay their eggs.

Diseases spread by mosquitoes can make people extremely ill.

DEADLIEST ANIMAL

It's hard to believe that the world's most dangerous animal is a mosquito. Some types of mosquito suck human blood and pass on diseases including malaria, yellow fever, the Zika virus, and dengue fever.

As a mosquito sucks up blood, its abdomen turns red

FREE FEED

It is only female mosquitoes that feed on blood. They have stabbing tube-like mouthparts, which they jab into their victim's skin. They pour a special liquid down one tube to keep the victim's blood flowing, while blood is sucked up through another tube.

Head hunters

Head lice are parasites with strong claws on their legs for gripping human hair.

One head louse can glue up to 10 eggs, or nits, to strands of hair every day, after feasting on blood.

The worst case of head lice recorded was on a child with 2,657 lice!

As it feeds, the tick expands. A tick full of blood can weigh up to **600** times as much as a hungry one!

DISEASE SPREADERS

The bloodsucking tsetse fly spreads sleeping sickness in Africa. Bed bugs spread the deadly Chagas disease in South America.

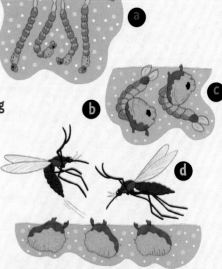

Bedbugs like human blood best. Thankfully they are rare in clean, well-aired homes.

Wrigglers and tumblers

Use your pond-dipping skills to catch some mosquito larvae and learn about their life cycles.

WHAT TO DO

1. Still, stagnant pond water, puddles, or rainwater in buckets are all good places to find mosquito larvae.

2. Keep the larvae in a jar of stagnant water. If it is greenish it will have enough food for the larvae to survive.

2

Things to notice:

a) See how the larvae hang upside down from the water surface, with breathing tubes poking out from their bottom ends. Watch how they wriggle.

b) Can you identify the head, thorax, and abdomen?

c) When the larvae are fully grown, they turn into pupae called tumblers. Can you see breathing trumpets on their heads?

d) After a few days, the tumblers molt and adult flying mosquitoes emerge.

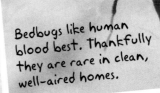

Always remember to wash your hands after pond-dipping!

Bug world

We need bugs. Without them, our world would change forever, because they are part of the planet's balance. Bugs help our plants grow, providing us — and other animals — with food. They also have some other useful benefits.

POLLINATION

When an insect visits a flower, it is attracted to the flower by its bright colors and sweet smells. Stripes on the petals guide the insects toward the sugary nectar in the center of the flower. As the insect feeds, it picks up the pollen on the flower's stamen.

A bee gets covered in a flower's pollen, and it also stores some on its legs.

FERTILIZATION

When an insect visits another flower, the pollen picked up from one flower brushes off onto the stigma of another. From here, it then fertilizes the flower's eggs. All flowering plants need to be fertilized before they can grow seeds, fruits, or nuts.

Ladybug

Bees are pollinators, but many other insects also do this important job as they move around a flower.

Flower cookies

Bees love flowers, and you can make these flower-shaped cookies to share.

SUPPLIES

flower cookie cutter or sharp knife • mixing bowl • wooden spoon • baking tray • greaseproof paper • wire rack • 3.5 ounces (100 g) soft butter • 3.5 ounces (100 g) caster sugar • 1 egg, lightly beaten • 9.7 ounces (275 g) plain flour • 1 teaspoon vanilla extract • colored icing, or icing ens

HOW TO MAKE

1. Turn the oven to 375°F (190°C), and line a baking tray with greaseproof paper.

2. Cream the butter and sugar together and add the egg and vanilla extract.

3. Stir the flour into the bowl and mix until it all comes together to make cookie dough.

4. Roll out the dough on a floured surface to a thickness of about 1 cm and use the cookie cutter (or a small, sharp knife) to cut flower shapes from the dough.

5. Place the cookies on the baking tray and cook for 8-10 minutes.

6. Let them cool on a wire rack before decorating with colored icing.

DECOMPOSITION

Without bugs, all the dead animals and plants in the world would pile up into one stinking mess. The bugs work with other living things, such as bacteria, mold, and mushrooms, to break up dead matter and return all the goodness to the soil. This is called decomposition and it makes the soil fertile, so more plants can grow.

Recyclers, such as ants, help to improve the soil.

Strange but true

Leafcutter ants can be used to close wounds. The ant bites the wound, then its body is ripped off, leaving its jaws in place.

Wart-biter bush crickets have been used to bite off warts, verrucas, and corns on human feet!

Greenbottle fly maggots feed on dying or dead flesh. Doctors can use them to treat wounds, cleaning them up and saving a person from a worsening infection.

INDEX

ACKNOWLEDGMENTS

The publishers would like to thank the following artists who have contributed to this book:

Cover Tracy Cottingham (The Bright Agency)

Insides Tom Heard, Stuart Jackson-Carter, Tim Loughhead

All other artwork is from the Miles Kelly Artwork Bank

The publishers would like to thank the following sources for the use of their photographs: t = top, c = center, b = bottom, l = left, r = right, bg = background

Alamy 16(bl) The Natural History Museum; 21(tr) Robert Henno Deposit 18(tl) lifeonwhite Diomedia 17(bl) The Natural History Museum FLPA 6(bl) Nigel Cattlin; 16(tl) Piotr Naskrecki, (c) Larry West; 17(c) Photo Researchers; 19(tl) Mitsuhiko Imamori/Minden Pictures Fotolia 4(bl) khz Getty 18(b) Torsten Blackwood Nature Picture Library 12(bl) Paul Harcourt Davies; 13(bl) Hans Christoph Kappel; 25(tr)

Nature Production; 26–27(bg) Ingo Arndt; 30(tr) Andy Sands Shutterstock.com 2–3(bg) Jorge Moro; 4(bg) Oleksandrum, (b) Potapov Alexander; 6–7(bg) Rob Hainer; 7(br) schankz; 10(cr) & 11(t), (c) Mathisa; 10(bc) tea maeklong, (c) KentaStudio; 12(bg) & 22–23(bg) Cathy Keifer; 17(tl) Patagonian Stock AE; 18(cr) feathercollector; 19(br) Marek Mierzejewski; 21(cl) kurt_G, (r) Khudolly; 23(c) Lyubov_Nazarova; 25(bl) Neale Cousland; 26(c) Jeff Caughey; 27(br) Alex Staroseltsev, (r) Ganibal; 28–29(bg) Kletr; 29(tr) Tobik, (tc) Risto0, (cr) jareynolds; 30(c) Marek Mierzejewski; 31(c) Humannet, (c) Piyavachara Nacchanandana, (bc) Eric Isselee Science Photo Library 13(b) B.G.Thomson; 19(c) Dennis Kunkel Microscopy; 23(c) Bjorn Rorslett Tom Murray 19(bl)

Every effort has been made to acknowledge the source and copyright holder of each picture. Miles Kelly Publishing apologizes for any unintentional errors or omissions.